REVOLUTION
FROM THE INSIDE OUT

BY
GREGORY DICKOW

REVOLUTION
From The Inside Out
©2010 by Gregory Dickow Ministries.
All rights reserved.

For information, please write
Gregory Dickow Ministries,
P.O. Box 7000
Chicago, IL 60680

or visit us online at www.changinglives.org.

TABLE OF CONTENTS

Introduction

A Life Changing Journey

Fasting from wrong thinking is a revolutionary concept that came to my heart at a time when I was frustrated by seeing so many people trying to change their lives, but getting little results.

This devotional, **Revolution—From the Inside Out**, is part of a uniquely-proven system of change that has helped elevate thousands to reach their God-given potential. Remember, its NOT a fast from food, but a fast from wrong thinking!

The way we think controls our entire life. Our thoughts shape our actions; our actions shape our habits; our habits shape our character; and our character shapes our destiny.

So, if we want to secure a satisfied and fulfilling destiny, it starts with our thoughts.

Its been said that it takes approximately 6 weeks to form a good habit or break a bad one. That's why I believe the Lord put on my heart to call people to a series of 40-day fasts from wrong thinking. Some of you are familiar with the first in this series of devotionals, "From the Inside Out". I have prepared this second volume because of the overwhelming response and amazing results. Simply put, it works.

And while 'fasting' from food has many benefits, our focus here is something entirely different and powerfully liberating. Over the next forty days, we will be fasting, or 'giving up' wrong ways of thinking.

This is the simplest and most effective form of change that you will ever experience…and it will produce life-long results.

Are you ready to replace the wrong thoughts that have limited you, with the unlimited possibilities of God?

Then lets begin…

Gregory Dickow

Day 1
I FEEL POWERLESS

**Today we are fasting from the thought that says:
I feel powerless.**

As we launch this 2nd volume of our fast from wrong think-ing, I'm asking the Lord to take us deeper into thinking pat-terns that will truly liberate us and establish a root system that will guarantee an abundant, fruitful life.

One of the greatest truths I have ever come to understand is that a "sense of powerlessness" is the root to all negative emotions. If you feel powerless to do anything about your past, you feel guilty. If you feel powerless to change your future, you feel afraid. And if you feel powerless to change your present, you feel depressed. When you feel like the people or things in your life will not change, you feel angry.

Depression, fear, guilt and anger are four of the most pow-erful negative emotions you will ever experience. And ALL of them stem from a sense of powerlessness. The thought that there's not much we can do about the economy or our weight or the allergies we grew up with, etc. imprisons us to accept and tolerate a mediocre and weak life.

CHANGE IT TODAY

1. **Embrace the truth that God has not given you a spirit of fear, but POWER, LOVE and a SOUND MIND** (2 Timothy 1:7). This is already done. You have this power in you.

2. **BELIEVE that power is in you.** Ephesians 3:20 says God is able to do exceeding abundantly above all you can ask or think ACCORDING TO THE POWER that is at work within you. There is power in you that enables God to do beyond what you can ask or think.

3. **Give God something to work with.** You have to THINK and ASK. Since He can do BEYOND, we have to at least give Him a base to begin with. We limit God when we don't think big and ASK big.

4. **Recognize and honor the Holy Spirit in you.** Acts 1:8 says, "You shall receive POWER when the Holy Spirit comes upon you..." Again, this power (dunamis=dynamite) is already in you. Thank God for the Holy Spirit in you. Romans 8:11 says, "the very same Spirit that raised Jesus from the dead lives in you."

5. **Take the limits off. Don't limit God.** Psalm 78:41 says that the children of Israel LIMITED the Lord. They limited Him, because they DID NOT REMEMBER His power (verse 42). We free God's hand to bless when we REMEMBER HIS PREVIOUS BLESSINGS. Psalm 103 says to not forget His benefits.

6. **EXPECT!** Never underestimate the power of expectation. Expect today for God's power to strengthen you; expect to be led by His Spirit today.

7. **Embrace your power:** the power to forgive and be forgiven (John 20:23); the power to heal (Mark 16:18); the power to speak the Word and get results. (Job 22:28).

THINK IT & SAY IT

I have God's POWER in my life right now. Through the Holy Spirit in me, I have the power to overcome sin, to change my life for the better, to be healed, to forgive, and to praise God no matter what, I have the power to speak God's Word and see His promises show up in my life.

I choose to remember what God has already done, which takes the limits off of my life and my expectations. I expect favor today, wisdom, understanding, and God's blessing!

Day 2
ANXIETY WHERE FINANCES ARE CONCERNED

I would like us to build upon yesterday's theme of power. Remember, most negative emotions come from a sense of powerlessness.

Today, particularly, it's on my heart to fast from thoughts of anxiety where finances are concerned. **When you feel powerless to get out of financial trouble, it will lead to anxiety, uncertainty, and worry.**

Crisis hotlines and therapists are being flooded by the surge in anxiety over finances. Studies show a strong connection between financial distress and emotional stress, depression, insomnia, migraines, and increased suicidal thoughts.

CHANGE IT TODAY

1. **Identify the specific things making you anxious.** Write them down. Pray, giving them over to God (Philippians 4:6-7).

2. **Believe there is a solution to whatever financial challenge you are facing.** BELIEVE there is a way out. You have to start by thinking this. Faith finds a way. There is a way!

3. **Ask God for wisdom** (James 1:5). The Bible also says that wisdom is MORE VALUABLE THAN silver and gold (Proverbs 8:11, Proverbs 3:15).

4. **Meditate on the people of scripture whom God provided for.** In Psalm 37:25, David said, "I was young, but now I am old, and I have NEVER seen

the righteous forsaken or His children begging for bread." Also, Genesis 24:1 says "and the Lord blessed Abraham in ALL THINGS." Expect this blessing in all things in your life. Why? Because you are the seed of Abraham (Galatians 3:29)!

5. **ASK GOD TO PROSPER YOU.** Folks, we have not because we ask not (James 4:1-2). Ask specifically for God to prosper you. Psalm 118:25 says, "O Lord, I beseech You, send prosperity now."

6. **Be covenant-minded.** A covenant is an agreement between 2 parties that says everything either has, is available to the other person. God has more than enough! And He says, "All that is Mine, is yours!" (Luke 15:31) Fill your mind with this covenant-thinking. He swore in His blood that He would provide for you. Believe He will.

7. **Continually think: "I have the power to get wealth."** Deuteronomy 8:17 says, "It is He that gives you the power to get wealth, SO THAT He may establish His covenant in the earth." Notice the PURPOSE of the POWER is to establish God's covenant in the earth. When that is your motive, great things are going to happen in your life. Again remember, thoughts of powerlessness lead to anxiety. You have the power!

8. **Focus on God's Kingdom and His purposes.** Matthew 6:33 says, "Seek first the Kingdom of God and His righteousness, and all these things will be added to you!"

THINK IT & SAY IT

I surrender my specific anxious thoughts to God. I believe there is a solution to my financial challenge. I am convinced that there is a way out.

I receive the wisdom of God, and expect that wisdom to empower me more than silver or gold...

I ask God to send prosperity, and I expect that He will. God will generously provide all that I need.

I choose to be covenant-minded, always expecting God, as my covenant partner, to find a way to get blessing in my hands.

I have been given, by God, the power to get wealth. That power is in me; therefore I'm free from anxiety, worry and fear. I don't have to add blessing to my life. It will follow me, as I focus on God and His kingdom!

Day 3

DEALING WITH THOUGHTS OF UNCERTAINTY

Today, I want us to deal with thoughts of uncertainty.

"What's going to happen in the world?" "What's going to happen in the economy?" "How's this going to affect my finances?" "I don't know what I'm going to do."

These thoughts of uncertainty in an unstable world must be dealt with.

Dependence upon this world's defective system, news and economy, creates uncertainty and fear.

In Genesis 26, there arose a great famine in the land. The first thing that God told Isaac was: DO NOT GO DOWN TO EGYPT.

"Egypt" represents the world's system apart from God. As long as we depend on this world's system, we will be uncertain and insecure in trying times.

Thinking that things will be OK if the "economy" turns around will breed uncertainty as well. We must not depend on this world's "economy." Listen to the original meaning of this word: "rules of the house."

Well, we're not playing by the rules of the world's house. We're playing by the rules of God's House! When we do, we will have absolute certainty and assurance.

CHANGE IT TODAY

1. **Renew your mind to God's system. The kingdom of God means His government, economy, system—the rules of the house!** Mark 4:26 says, "The Kingdom of God is like a man who casts seed into the ground." Live by the system of sowing and reaping.

2. **Realize that you can determine your future by the seeds you sow.** Sow faith seeds. Sow word seeds. Sow praise seeds. Sow financial seeds. As you do, assurance and confidence will fill your heart.

3. **Expect God to lead you by the Holy Spirit.** John 16:13 says the Spirit of Truth will reveal to you the things to come. Just as God showed Joseph that famine would come, just as He showed the Magi to go a different way because Herod would try to kill them in Matthew 2:1-12, He will show you as well.

4. **God is no respecter of persons.** What He did for others, He will do for you. You must fill your mind with this truth and expect Him to lead you (Acts 10: 34, 35; Eph. 6: 9; Col. 3: 25; I Pet. 1: 17).

5. **You can be certain that He called you and chosen you; therefore you will not stumble** (2 Peter 1:10). Tell yourself that.

6. **Pray in the Holy Spirit.** When we don't know what to pray, the Spirit helps our weaknesses and prays for us in our inner man, as we yield to His language. Romans 8:26 tells us praying in the Spirit means praying the Word, praying with praise, and praying with the beautiful gift of tongues. Look up this awesome verse in the Message Translation: Romans 8:26-28, "If we don't know how or what to pray, it doesn't matter.

He does our praying in and for us, making prayer out of our wordless sighs, our aching groans. He knows us far better than we know ourselves..."

THINK IT & SAY IT

I can be certain in uncertain times. I am not connected to the economy of this world—the rules of their house. I am connected to God's economy—the rules of His house. I live by the system of sowing and reaping. I can be certain about the future by sowing the seeds of God's Word.

I am led by the Spirit of God. He will reveal to me the things to come, so I can prepare accordingly and be victorious no matter what comes. Just as He led men and women in Scripture, He will lead me, since He is no respecter of persons.

I am called and chosen by God, and therefore, I will not stumble. When I don't know what to do, I will trust the Holy Spirit and allow Him to pray through me—bringing me into the perfect will of God no matter what is going on in this world, in Jesus' Name!

DEPENDING ON OTHER PEOPLE FOR OUR NEEDS

One of the rules of the world's house that we must fast from is our dependence upon others.

Remember, the word "economy" means "rules of the house." We are either living by the world's "rules of the house" or by God's.

We need one another to complete the purpose of God in the world, but we don't need to depend on other people coming through for us for our needs.

CHANGE IT TODAY

1. **God will provide.** Philippians 4:19 says He provides **all our needs** according to His riches and glory. Renew your mind to the fact that He provides for ALL our needs, not just finances.

2. **Dependence upon others is NOT humility, it's misplaced trust**. Psalm 43:5 says, "Why so downcast, O my soul? Put your hope in God." David is saying that when we put our hope in people, in government, in the world's 'rules of the house,' we will wind up depressed and downcast. Shift your trust and hope to God. Trust that He will direct your path.

3. **Meditate on Romans 5:5** ..."Hope does not disappoint BECAUSE the love of God has been shed abroad in our hearts by the Holy Spirit." There is a hope that will never disappoint you—Hope in God's promise and provision.

4. **Realize that over-dependency upon others keeps you from loving them.** When you depend on someone doing for you or coming through for you, you can't love them. Therefore you can't succeed, because love never fails. You can't love them, because you need them too much. Love gives. Love doesn't depend on others to give.

5. **Stop striving to get the things you need.** God wants to provide for YOU! Realize God humbles you by FEEDING YOU. Deuteronomy 8:3 says **"He humbled you... and fed you with manna which you did not know nor did your fathers know..."**

6. **Don't trust the provision, trust the provider.** Deuteronomy 8:3a says "...that He might make you know that man shall not live by bread alone..."

7. **USE THE WORD to REALLY LIVE!** Deuteronomy 8:3b says, "...but man lives by every word that proceeds from the mouth of the Lord."

THINK IT & SAY IT

God will provide for ALL MY NEEDS. I live by God's ECONOMY—the rules of His house.

I free myself from dependence upon others, and I will depend on God, empowering me to love others freely. My trust and hope is in God. And THAT hope will never let me down, because God's love is in me, and He will never disappoint me.

I stop fighting to get the things I need. I believe God wants to provide for me. He will feed me, and I choose to receive it and fully accept His help.

I will not put my trust in what I have, but in the One who provides. My every need comes from every Word that comes from the mouth of God, in Jesus' Name!"

Day 5

FORGIVENESS IS NOT THAT BIG OF A DEAL

Today we begin fasting from thoughts of unforgiveness.

I know we don't come out and say it, but in our minds, I believe many people allow unresolved conflict and bitter feelings to remain in them, without realizing how much it robs us of the life God wants us to enjoy.

Forgiveness is the gateway to so much of God's blessing in our lives, just as unforgiveness is a gateway into so much negative in our lives.

An unforgiving heart is poison to your spirit, soul and body. Hebrews 12:15 says that a root of bitterness springs up and defiles many. It doesn't just defile many other people, but it defiles MANY OTHER AREAS OF OUR LIFE.

The thought that forgiveness is optional, or that we can get around to it when we get a chance, has to be eliminated from our mindsets.

CHANGE IT TODAY

1. **Faith works through forgiveness**—One of the most important verses about faith is in Mark 11:24 which says, "All things for which you pray and ask, believe that you have received them, and they shall be granted." But notice what it says next...

2. **Mark 11:25 says, "And when you stand praying, if you hold anything against anyone, forgive him..."** So you see, forgiveness is the gateway to answered prayer.

3. **Deal with it today.** Ephesians 4:26 says, "don't let the sun go down on your anger." There's a reason that we need to forgive and be forgiven BEFORE

the sun goes down. **Our hearts are not designed to carry grudges longer than a day. This is why so many people are weighed down with stress, anger and depression.** A relationship is unresolved. A heart is hardened. A bitter feeling is being carried into our tomorrow.

4. **Accept the fact that you were forgiven BECAUSE of the blood of Jesus.** Therefore, forgive others for the same reason—not because they deserved it. Forgiveness is a gift.

5. **Forgiveness is the gateway to our inheritance** (Acts 26:18). As we realize we are forgiven, we experience His blessing and inheritance in our lives. As we forgive others, we empower them to experience it too.

6. **YOU HAVE THE POWER TO FORGIVE.** God gave us the Holy Spirit, so that we could forgive as He did. In John 20:22-23 it says, "He breathed on them and said, 'receive the Holy Spirit. Whoever sins you forgive are forgiven, and whoever sins you retain are retained'." When you forgive someone's sins, then you shine the light of God's grace upon their darkened heart, enabling them to see that God really IS good, that He loves them, and that He wants to share His life with them.

THINK IT & SAY IT

My faith works because I refuse to hold anything against anyone. When I pray, I choose to forgive because forgiveness is the gateway to answered prayer.

I refuse to let the poison of unforgiveness defile me and others around me. I will not let a day go by where I hold bitter feelings in my heart toward anyone.

I accept the blood of Jesus as the only way to be forgiven, and I extend forgiveness to others through that same blood. I have the power to forgive others through the Holy Spirit in me. I release, this day, every person who I have ever held anything against. I am free and so are they! In Jesus' Name.

Day 6

"I TRIED TO FORGIVE, BUT I JUST DON'T FEEL IT."

Today we're fasting from the thought that says, "I tried to forgive, but I just don't feel it."

Many people are held back in life because they are waiting for the feeling of forgiveness before they let go. In the meantime, the unforgiveness continues its damage against them, while they wait for their feelings to change.

The problem with this thinking is that it is backwards.

CHANGE IT TODAY

1. **Forgiveness is not a feeling.** It is a decision. Whatever grudge, bitterness, or resentment that you have toward someone will not go away without a choice to let it go.

2. **Forgive by faith.** 2 Corinthians 5:7 says we live by faith, we forgive by faith. That means that when you forgive someone out loud, from your heart, you must believe that it is done. Never let your faith follow your feelings. Your feelings will catch up with your faith.

3. **Don't be fooled by the feelings of resentment or anger when they try to come back.** You'll be tempted to think, "I don't feel anything, so nothing has changed. I guess I must not have truly forgiven." This is a lie! This is the thought you must fast from.

4. **Maintain an attitude of thankfulness that you have been set free from the pain and consequence of unforgiveness.** Thank God that you are free and

healed. As you do this EVERY TIME that you feel those feelings, you will feel less and less of the pain, until it vanishes forever.

5. **Understand the meaning of the word: FOR-GIVE.** It simply means to GIVE, BEFORE. We need to "give" forgiveness, BEFORE the person apologizes, BEFORE they change, and most importantly BEFORE you feel anything. Just as faith works by believing God's promises BEFORE they show up, (Mark 11:24-25), forgiveness works BEFORE you feel it. When you forgive BEFORE you feel good feelings about that person, you are living in the highest level of faith. And this is pleasing to God (Hebrews 11:6).

6. **Meditate on what God has done FOR you, rather than what people have done TO you.** Psalm 103:2-4 says, "Bless the Lord O my soul and forget none of his benefits—He pardons all your iniquities, heals all your diseases, redeems your life from destruction, crowns you with loving-kindness and compassion."

THINK IT & SAY IT

I accept that forgiveness is not a feeling. It is a decision. I expect the bitter feelings, the problems, the unanswered prayers to change beginning today because of the choice I have made.

I forgive by faith, which means that as I act on the Word of God and declare my forgiveness out loud, I am pleasing to God, whether I feel something or not.

I am forgiven and I am a forgiver! I choose to forgive others (AND MYSELF), BEFORE they change, before they deserve it, and before I feel it. I focus on what God has done for me, rather than what others have done to me, and therefore, I am free. In Jesus' Name!

Day 7

"IF I FORGIVE, I'LL BE TAKEN ADVANTAGE OF."

Today we are fasting from the thought that says: **"If I forgive, I'll be taken advantage of."**

It is very tempting to give in to this false belief, but don't give in to that thinking. Forgiveness doesn't mean tolerance. If someone is hurting you, don't remain a punching bag for their mistreatment.

If you've been abused, you don't continue accepting it. Get in a safe place.

But, all of us need to trust God, regardless of what has been done to us.

CHANGE IT TODAY

1. **Remember Joseph**—thrown into the pit by his brothers, then sold into slavery. Bitterness could have eaten him alive, and would have, but he had something BETTER going for him.

2. **Believe God is with you** in your situation. Genesis 39:2 said HE PROSPERED BECAUSE GOD WAS WITH HIM.

3. **Prosperity is about who is with you.** Joseph prospered because GOD WAS WITH HIM. David prospered because God was with him. Psalm 27:3 says, "though an army encamp against me, I will not fear..." Why? Because Psalm 118:6 says, "The Lord is on my side, therefore I will not fear what man can do to me." God is with you, and He is on your side.

4. **Believe that NO WEAPON FORMED AGAINST YOU CAN PROSPER.** (Isaiah 54:17) This is why most people struggle with forgiving others. They think that what

that person did can truly hurt them. Yet the Bible says, "NOTHING SHALL BY ANY MEANS HURT YOU." (Luke 10:19)

5. **Declare with Joseph:** "You meant evil against me, **but God** meant it for good". I love those 2 words in the scripture: BUT GOD. You see, no matter what they did to Joseph, BUT GOD. No matter what the devil tries to do to you, BUT GOD. No matter what mistakes have been made by you or against you, BUT GOD. See God as the INTERRUPTER of people's sins against you. He is the interrupter of the devil's plots against you.

6. **EVEN IF MAN DECIDES** to hurt you or rob you of the best part of your life, **nothing can prevail against what God has destined** for those who love Him—Romans 8:28, 1 Corinthians 2:9. FORGIVENESS releases God's power to convert even the most sinister plots against you into good. **JOSEPH BECAME 2nd in command to Pharaoh, saving the world from famine, because He forgave.**

7. **Believe that forgiveness, though it may not change the past, will open up an incredible future.**

THINK IT & SAY IT

What others have done to me has no power over me or my future. My future is determined by my choices, including my choice to forgive.

What others have done to me cannot hurt me. Nothing shall by any means hurt me. What they meant against me, God turns around for my good. I expect God to interrupt all plots, weapons, and sins against me.

Through forgiveness, I release God's power to convert all wrong against me into good. I believe that my attitude and action of forgiveness will open up an amazing future for me, in Jesus' name!

Day 8

"I JUST CAN'T FORGIVE MYSELF"

Today I want to share one more thought regarding the subject of forgiveness—however, this time, we are fasting from the thought that says: **"I just can't forgive myself."**

Who hasn't thought that at one time or another? The devil would love to keep us in self-condemnation for the things we have done or failed to do. He knows it paralyzes us and prevents us from making the kind of impact that God intended for us.

I recently read of a young teenager who accidentally struck his 5 year old sister with a car, tragically killing her in their driveway. And as tragic as it is for a child to die in that way at such a young age, the greater tragedy is the difficulty this young man will have forgiving himself. Though few of us have faced something as dramatic as this, we all need to overcome the thoughts that try to accuse us for what we have done. Perhaps this message will get to that young man and provide the encouragement he will need in this challenging time.

Let's beat this thought into the ground—hasn't it beaten us long enough?

CHANGE IT TODAY

1. **Realize that we only deserve forgiveness because of the blood of Jesus.** Not because what we did wrong "never happened," or it wasn't that bad. Give up rationalizations and excuses.

2. **It *was* that bad, but God is even MORE good!** James 2:13 says mercy triumphs over judgment. His mercy toward you TRUMPS your judgment over yourself. Believe that God is bigger than what you did. In Luke 22, Peter denied the Lord 3 times, and Jesus forgave him. Later, Peter preached the first sermon after Jesus rose from the dead, and 3000 people were saved in a day! Peter was able to forgive himself when he knew Jesus had accepted him. In the same way, realize that you have been accepted by God, no matter what you have done, simply by believing in the work of the cross of Jesus Christ.

3. **Give up your right to hold ANYTHING against yourself that God does not hold against you**. If God can forgive you, you can forgive yourself. His standard is absolute perfection, and He forgives you. Psalm 103:12 says, "As far as east is from west, so far has He removed our transgressions from us."

4. **Stop rehearsing what you did.** It's done. It's over. Now accept the 2nd chance that God offers. Philippians 3:13 says "forgetting what lies behind, and reaching forward..."

5. **Believe that guilt doesn't come from God.** He doesn't impose guilt on you to try to get you to stop doing something. Romans 2:4 says it is His lovingkindness that leads us to repentance.

6. **Give up the SELF-PUNISHMENT**. Some people have said to themselves: "I'll make myself feel bad to pay for what has been done." Why should we pay the price that has ALREADY been paid for what we've done wrong? Stop beating yourself up—The fact is, whatever you have done that you can't seem to forgive yourself for is already forgiven. By trying to "pay for what we have done," we are insulting the very blood of Jesus that HAS PAID the price in full.

THINK IT & SAY IT

I receive mercy today, because of the blood of Jesus. Though I didn't deserve it, God proclaims over me that I am "not guilty". Where I have failed, God's mercy triumphs over judgment.

I give up my right today to hold ANYTHING against myself— I deserve to be punished, but Jesus took THAT punishment for me. I forget what lies behind and press on, moving forward in my life with God, even though I feel like I have blown it beyond repair.

I reject this guilt and self-condemnation that the devil is trying to put on me. God is the God of 2nd chances. I will no longer try to make myself feel bad to pay for what has been done. The price for what I did or failed at has been paid in full by God! In Jesus' name!

Day 9

"It's Just Not Fair. God's Not Fair."

Today we are 'fasting' from the thought that says: "It's just not fair. God's not fair."

We've all wondered, why does one person prosper, while another struggles to just get by? One person lives to be 100, another tragically dies at 16. One parent has a perfectly healthy child, while another has a child who is constantly ill or diseased. What about some being born in a bountiful land such as America, while others are born in a devastated country?

Folks, we live in a fallen world, affected by the sin of Adam and Eve, and thrown out of kilter from God's original plan. As a result, imperfect health, weather, imperfect DNA, air, etc., has permeated the earth. We are all born with imperfect circumstances—some obvious, and some more subtle; but God gives us all a NEW BEGINNING the day we are born again. Until that time, unfairness and imbalance will remain. But in JESUS CHRIST, God's goodness and fairness is made available to everyone.

Let's fast from the thinking that God is not fair, and life is not fair.

CHANGE IT TODAY

1. **God's promises are available to whosoever believes.**
   (John 3:16) It's been said, every cloud has a silver lining—well, every problem has a promise from God to overcome it (2 Corinthians 1:20). There is a promise for every problem, for every tragedy, for everything we will ever face. Believe it!

2. **Overcome what's in front of you**. You don't have anyone else's battles. You only have to win the battle right in front of you.

3. **Recognize the nearness of God. He is present with you. Psalm 73:28 NASB says, "But as for me, the near**ness of God is my good...." It wasn't fair what Joseph's brothers did to him, but God was with him, and he overcame. (Genesis 39:1-2) Your trial or trouble or tragedy is no match for God's presence. Trust in His name: Jehovah Shammah, the Lord is with you.

4. **Expect God will right every wrong.** (Romans 12:19) He will avenge His children who have suffered unfairly (Luke 18:8).

5. **Overcome evil with good** (Romans 12:21). You must see the inequities (those things that have happened in life that weren't fair) as opportunities to make a difference. Do something good every time you feel something unfair has been done to you.

6. **Don't be afraid.** Genesis 15:1 AMP says, "Fear not Abraham, I am your shield, your ABUNDANT COMPENSATION. Your reward shall be great!" Remember, you have a covenant with God (Galatians 3:29). If you belong to Christ, you are Abraham's seed. Whatever He did for Abraham, He has promised He will do for you!

THINK IT & SAY IT

No matter what has happened in my life, God has given me promises to overcome it. His promises are to whoso-ever believes, and that means me! I am a believer, not a doubter.

I refuse to measure what's fair by comparison to others. I overcome what's right in front of me with the Word of God.

God's presence is with me and in me. What I am facing right now is no match for the presence of God.

I trust God to right every wrong. He will avenge the wrong that has been done to me. He will turn it around for good.

I choose to overcome evil with good. Therefore, no matter how unfair things may have seemed, God will make up for whatever has been lost. He is my abundant compensation. I have a covenant with God, and therefore whatever He did for Abraham, He will do for me as well, In Jesus' Name!

Day 10
"It's Just Not Fair. God's Not Fair," Part II

Yesterday we began fasting from the thought, "It's not fair. God's not fair."

Our concept of God shapes how we view ourselves, our life, and those around us. A wrong concept of God also shapes our expectations. If we believe He is weak, then we will not expect His power in our lives. If we believe He is distant and uncaring, then we will not expect His intervention in our time of need.

When you discover what He is really like, you become invincible. Daniel 11:32 declares, "Those who KNOW their God shall be strong and do exploits." When you see Him for who He is, you realize there is nothing He wouldn't do for you. You realize that when life isn't fair, God is still good, and He knows how to make up for whatever wrong has been done by you or against you.

Let's continue to obliterate the thought that says "it's not fair." And ...

CHANGE IT TODAY

1. **Believe in the God of restoration.** Joel 2:23-25 says, "I will restore to you the years that have been eaten." No matter how unfair life has been to you, God is in the restoration business. He will make up to you for lost time, if you believe this promise. Get this in your thinking: He will restore YEARS!

2. **Meditate on Psalm 23:6** which says, "Surely goodness and mercy will FOLLOW you all the days of your life. Think on this word: SURELY. It leaves no doubt, no question. IT WILL HAPPEN.

3. **See things through the eyes of eternity.** (Colossians 3:1-4) The poem goes: "Only one life will soon be past—only what's done for Christ will last." Live with eternal purpose. Measure your choices by how they will affect eternity, and how important they are to heaven. The rest of the poem goes: "And when I'm dying, how happy I'll be, if the lamp of my life has burned out FOR THEE."

4. **Realize misfortune and disappointment don't have control over you.** It's how you respond to these things that determines the outcome of your life—both here on earth and in eternity.

5. **FOCUS on the good God has done in your life.** (Psalm 103:1-5) RECOGNIZE what you've been given is a gift to serve others with (1 Peter 4:10). Use what God has done in your life to bring others to a higher place in God.

6. **Promotion comes from above** (Psalm 75:7). No matter how far down life has tried to put you, no matter how far down the devil has tried to push you, God is the God of promotion. He will raise you up, if you trust Him. He will exalt you, as you humble yourself. Humility accepts what God says (James 1:21). Expect to be raised up above the unfair treatment this life brings.

THINK IT & SAY IT

I believe in the God of restoration. He will restore to me all the years that have been destroyed in my life, by the devil, by how I've been treated, and by my bad decisions. I expect goodness and mercy to follow me ALL the days of my life. It will SURELY happen.

I choose to live with eternal purpose. What I do for Jesus is what will echo in eternity—that's how I choose to live.

The outcome of my life is determined by the choices I make—and my choices will line up with God's Word.

I expect promotion to come to my life, because I humble myself and receive what God says about me. No matter what this life tries to bring me, God will raise me up above it. He is more than fair. He is more than enough. And when life's not fair, God more than makes up for it in my life, in Jesus' Name!

Day 11
"I Don't Believe It"

Today we are fasting from the thought that says, "I don't believe it!" Or "I can't believe that."

This is the language and vocabulary of hell itself, trying to penetrate your mind. There are 3 primary things that the devil doesn't want you to believe:

1. That God's Word is true AND works.

2. That you have authority over the devil.

3. That God is good, and the author of ONLY good.

It's vital that we make sure our thinking lines up with the word of God concerning faith and believing. For example, if you believe that EVERYTHING that happens in life was pre-destined by God, then you will lower your defenses against the devil. And Satan would love for you to just accept whatever comes in life as God's will. This requires no faith, no battle, and leads to no victory.

CHANGE IT TODAY

1. **Take charge of your garden!** Your heart is your garden. Proverbs 4:20 says, "Watch over your heart with all diligence, for out of it flow the issues of life." Adam was responsible for the Garden of Eden when Satan crept in through his deceptive lies. It was Adam's responsibility to drive that snake out of his garden. Because he was passive and tolerant of Satan's thoughts in his garden, his life was ruined!

2. **Do not for a moment submit to the thought that the devil has power over you!** Jesus said in Luke 10:19, "Behold I give you authority to tread upon serpents (devils) and scorpions and over ALL the POWER OF THE ENEMY. And nothing shall by any means hurt you." This is power that money can't buy, education can't acquire, human strength can't achieve. This is heavenly power that is irrefutable.

3. **Exercise your authority over the devil** the same way Jesus did. He spoke the Word of God (Matthew 4:4, Luke 4:4).

4. **Hold on to the Word of God.** Satan always comes after the Word. In Genesis, he talked Adam and Eve out of believing what God said. There's nothing new under the sun. In Mark 4:15 he comes immediately to steal the word. Hide the Word in your heart and it will give you victory whenever necessary (Psalm 119:9-11).

5. **Understand spiritual warfare**. The devil does everything he can to convince you that the Word isn't true or won't work. That's why 1 Timothy 6:12 says, "Fight the good fight of faith." The battle we're in is the battle to believe. But nothing is impossible for those who believe. And God is watching over His Word to perform it.

6. **Believe in the faithfulness of God.** 1 Thessalonians 5:24, "Faithful is He who called you, and He will bring it to pass!" Think on His faithfulness. Life will present its share of problems, but God is faithful. He called you. He will bring His calling to pass. Our job is to believe.

7. **Expect supernatural peace and joy in your life.** Romans 15:13 says joy and peace abound in your life THROUGH believing. As you are believing what God says, peace will fill your heart. Joy will fill your heart.

THINK IT & SAY IT

I take charge of my garden by watching over my heart. I will not be passive or tolerant of Satan's thoughts. I have authority over the devil, and I exercise that authority by speaking the Word of God.

I fight the fight of faith by believing what God says, and I refuse to accept anything less than the promises of God's Word. I believe in the faithfulness of God and trust that He will bring His promises to pass in my life.

I expect supernatural peace and joy in my life by focusing my faith on believing what God said. I take control over doubt by filling my mind and mouth with the Word of God.

Day 12

"I MUST BE OUT OF GOD'S WILL."

Today we are fasting from the thought: "I must be out of God's will." And the thoughts that go with it:

What if I miss God's will? What if I make the wrong decision?

These are some of the thoughts that punish many people; that produce doubt, uncertainty and fear in us, almost becoming self-fulfilling prophecies leading us to make bad decisions.

CHANGE IT TODAY

1. **Put first things first.** God's "will" is His Word. ("Testament" means "will") It's not a mystery. If you left a "will" for your loved ones, it would focus on what you are doing for them, rather than what they need to do for you (Of course, you would be dead!). FOCUS ON WHAT GOD HAS DONE. Read the "will" or the "testament", as if it were listing what NOW belongs to you since Jesus died and rose again. (Hebrews 9:14-20)

2. **The "will" of God begins with a "state of being" not a "state of doing."** What I mean by this is: since our foundational scripture is "As a man thinks, so is he" (Proverbs 23:7), our focus should be on what God said we ARE. Then, that will produce what God wants us to DO. When you know you ARE what God says you are, then you will DO the will of God. The right decisions will be the by-product of the right thinking.

3. **As you fill your heart up with the Word of God, He will lead you safely into His will!** Psalm 119:9-11 says, "I have hidden your Word in my heart that I might not SIN against Thee." "Sin" = missing the mark. You won't MISS the "will" or the mark when you hide the Word in your heart!

4. **The will of God is activated in our lives through the giving of thanks.** 1 Thessalonians 5:18 says, "In everything give thanks, for this is the WILL OF GOD for you, in Christ Jesus." Notice, He doesn't say "give thanks FOR everything," but rather, "give thanks IN everything." No matter what you are facing right now, the will of God is to give thanks, IN the midst of it. By giving thanks and praise CONTINUALLY, we are invading our situation with the presence and possibilities of God's power!

5. **The will of God is bigger and broader than most people think.** At a large airport, there are several runways that a plane can land on, safely arriving at its destination. Get rid of the mindset that there's only one runway and you might miss it and crash! There are several runways in the will of God, and therefore many options that are equally acceptable and approved by God.

THINK IT & SAY IT

I am not going to miss God's will for my life! His Word is His Will, and I accept and embrace His Word as the cornerstone of my life.

I AM what God's Word says I am. I have a covenant with God that will lead me into the right decisions for my life. He will keep me in His Will, as I keep His Word in my heart.

I choose a life of thanks and praise which puts me in the middle of God's will, AND brings God's will into the middle of my situation, in Jesus' Name!

Day 13

"I Must Be Out Of God's Will." (Part II)

Today, we are continuing to fast from the thought: "What if I miss the will of God?" (Part II)

For centuries, good-hearted believers have feared missing the will of God for their lives. People have struggled and strived to know the will of God and hope they could discover this eternal mystery.

Let's dispel this myth. The will of God is NOT a mystery.

CHANGE IT TODAY

1. **NOW (right now) abide these three: faith, hope and love—but the greatest of these is love (1 Corinthians 13:3).** This really simplifies it for us. I am in the will of God when I am abiding in FAITH, HOPE and LOVE. When I am believing what God said, I am in faith. This puts me in the will of God. Adam and Eve fell short of God's will WHEN they believed something OTHER than what God said.

2. **Next, I am in the will of God when I am abiding in hope.** Hope is expectation of good. When I am expecting good from God every day, I am in the will of God. Psalm 118:24 says, "This is the day the Lord has made, I will rejoice and be glad in it!"

3. **AND, I am in the will of God when I am abiding in love.** Everything comes together in our lives when we believe the love that God has for us. The greatest commandment—love God with all your heart and love your neighbor as yourself—this is the will of God.

This all begins with believing the love God has toward us. 1 John 4:16 NASB: "We have come to know and have believed the love which God has for us. God is love..."

4. **He will not leave you hanging!** Job 33:14 AMPLIFIED says, "For God [does reveal His will; He] speaks not only once, but more than once..." See, He isn't going to make it hard and laborious for you to know His will. He will speak more than once, to get the point across to you. That's why there are 66 books in the Bible! That's why we should be hearing the Word over and over in our minds, in our churches, in every way we can! **Expect God to reveal His will to you today!**

5. **Commit your life into His hands.** Proverbs 16:3 AMPLIFIED says, "Roll your works upon the Lord [commit and trust them wholly to Him; He will cause your thoughts to become agreeable to His will, and] so shall your plans be established and succeed."

6. **Be willing to do it, BEFORE you know it.** John 17:7 (NASB) says, "If anyone is willing to do His will, he will know of the teaching, whether it is of God or whether I speak from Myself."

THINK IT & SAY IT

I am in the will of God because I abide in faith, hope and love. I believe what God said, I expect good from God today, and I believe the love God has for me. God will not leave me hanging. He will reveal His will to me over and over.

I commit my works and my ways to Him, and He will cause my thoughts to come into agreement with His will. I expect to be established today and succeed. I pray and receive God's will in my life, today, as it is in heaven, in Jesus' Name!

Day 14

"I FEEL LIKE A FAKE; I FEEL LIKE A HYPOCRITE."

Today, we are fasting from the thought: "I feel like a fake; I feel like a hypocrite."

For centuries, the devil has been weaving defeat and condemnation into people's minds by getting them to feel like they're not really saved, or they're saved, but they're not the person they pretend to be in public. Stop letting the devil rob you of your joy and peace through this lie.

We all at times have felt like hypocrites. We say we believe, then we sometimes doubt. We say we love God, but feel at times numb. We are supposed to "walk in love," but we feel like hurting someone sometimes. Anybody been there besides me?

Paul the apostle knew this battle, and today we're going to join him in victory.

He said, "For I know that nothing good dwells in me, that is, in my flesh; for the willing is present in me, but the doing of the good is not." (Romans 7:18)

CHANGE IT TODAY

1. **Recognize the battle that you're in.** Your spirit (inner man) is holy and wants to do what's right. Your flesh, however, doesn't. One translation said, "I have the desire to do what's right, but I cannot carry it out." Before we're done, your spirit is going to win this battle!

2. **Realize that you're not alone in the battle.** EVERYONE deals with this. The fact that you realize you want to obey God, but are honest enough to admit you often fail, is NOT hypocrisy. It's "truth in your innermost

being." (Psalm 51:6) **The part of you that doesn't want to obey God is not the real you – it's your flesh.**

3. **Don't worry about what other people think of you.** Only the "self-righteous" think they have it all together. Look to Jesus as your High Priest. That means, He goes to God with His blood and says, "Father, this one has been cleansed by My blood. This is your child, and they are holy NOW because they are washed." He goes to the Father on our behalf and paves the way for us to be forgiven, accepted, and righteous—IN HIM.

4. **Take off the mask.** You don't have to be "Miss Perfect" or "Mr. Always has it together." There's something liberating about not having to pretend you have it all together. That doesn't mean you go out and sin deliberately. It means you humbly admit, like Paul the apostle in Romans 7:19, "For the good which I have a mind to do, I do not: but the evil which I have no mind to do, that I end up doing." He's not making a bad confession here. He's making an honest one. THEN...

5. **Declare your victory in Christ!** Romans 7:22-23 Message Translation says, "I truly delight in God's commands, but it's pretty obvious that not all of me joins in that delight."

6. **It's OK to need a Savior!** Paul asked: Who can deliver me from this condition? Romans 7:25 says, "The answer, thank God, is that JESUS CHRIST CAN AND DOES..."

7. **We walk by faith, not by sight.** 2 Corinthians 5:7 You can serve God, now, even when you feel like a fake. Believe what God says about you, and don't bow down to what your flesh and the devil try to tell you about your weaknesses, contradictions and mistakes.

THINK IT & SAY IT

I recognize that I am in a battle between my spirit and my flesh. I will no longer give into the lie that I'm a fake or a hypocrite. I have a flesh trying to control me;, but my spirit truly wants to obey God. I yield today, to my spirit, by yielding to GOD'S WORD.

Jesus Christ has delivered me from the wickedness of my past and my flesh. I am forgiven. Everything in me that doesn't want to obey God IS NOT THE REAL ME. The real me is made in the image of God and is more than a conqueror through Jesus Christ my Lord!

Day 15
"I Just Don't Have What It Takes"

Have you ever felt like that? You don't have what it takes to be a Christian, you just don't have what it takes to be a good parent, to stop sinning, to overcome the devil and temptation. Perhaps you've thought that you didn't have what it takes to be promoted at your job, or to get the job you need, or to be the spouse you're supposed to be.

In fact, this thought "I just don't have what it takes," is a quote right out of the Bible (Message translation). **In Romans 7:17-20, Paul says: "I need something...I realize I don't have what it takes... something has gone wrong deep within me and gets the better of me every time."**

We often fall short and then embrace defeat. REMEMBER, there is no stopping the man or woman who is set free from wrong thinking.

Paul gives us insight into the struggle we all face, and then reveals the secret to being set free. True freedom and true victory come from being free from wrong thinking.

CHANGE IT TODAY

1. **EMBRACE YOUR FREEDOM FROM CONDEMNATION.**
   The first step toward breaking out of this defeated mindset is to realize that even when you've fallen short or messed up, GOD DOES NOT CONDEMN YOU. The Apostle Paul comes right out of Romans 7, and declares in Romans 8:1 "There is NOW therefore NO condemnation, for those who are in Christ Jesus..." Has something gone wrong deep within you, like Paul? Well, don't be condemned about it. God has just the remedy!

2. **Believe in the patience of God toward you.** When you realize how patient He is, you'll be more patient with yourself. Remember, He's STILL WORKING ON YOU! Philippians 1:6 says, "Faithful is He who began the good work in you, and He will complete it until the day of Jesus Christ!" Time is on your side. He will never give up on you until His work is done!

3. **Start with what you have!** David said in Psalm 103, "Bless the Lord O my soul, and all that is within me... who pardons all my sins, heals all my diseases, redeems my life from destruction..." He started listing what he already had in his life. Before you go grocery shopping, look in your cupboard! There's more there than you realize! But notice also:

4. **Tell yourself what you DO HAVE.** Philemon verse 6 says, "Your faith becomes effective through acknowledging what is already in you, in Christ Jesus." This verse is so liberating. Our faith overcomes our flesh and the devil by acknowledging what we already have.

5. **YOU HAVE THE HELPER—THE HOLY SPIRIT LIVING INSIDE YOU.** Romans 8:11 says that the SAME SPIRIT that raised Jesus from the dead dwells in you. How's that for HAVING WHAT IT TAKES. If you have the person who has what it takes to resurrect the dead, LIVING IN YOU, then you have what it takes to do AND to overcome ANYTHING.

6. **You have the mind of Christ** (1 Corinthians 2:16). God's thoughts are not beyond you. You are not separated from God anymore. He lives in you. His thoughts are in you. As you read His Word, you realize how He thinks, and that is the gateway to your new way of thinking.

THINK IT & SAY IT

Even when I've fallen short, sinned and felt like a failure, I AM NOT CONDEMNED. I am in Christ and I am free. God is patient with me and will finish what He started. I recognize what He has put in me.

When I feel like I don't have what it takes, I realize the greatest power in the universe lives in me! I DO HAVE WHAT IT TAKES. It takes the Holy Spirit, and He lives in me. He is my helper! (John 14:16, John 15:26, John 16:7) It takes the mind of Christ, and I have it! I have everything I need and amply supplied— My God supplies, and I will never lack what it takes again, in Jesus' Name!

Day 16
"I'M AFRAID"

Today we're fasting from the granddaddy of all wrong thinking: "I'm afraid."

Fear is at the root of just about every negative thing that happens in our lives. We're afraid of failing, afraid of being alone, or rejected, afraid of running out of money, afraid that people will let us down, that we won't find a spouse, or a job, and the list goes on and on. All fear is rooted in the core belief that God's Word won't work. For example, the fear of not having enough is rooted in the fear that Philippians 4:19 isn't true. If you believe that "God will supply all your needs according to His riches..." then fear leaves.

CHANGE IT TODAY

1. **Meditate on the fact that God's Word is true.** In John 17:17 Jesus said, "Thy Word is truth." What God says is fact—whether you feel it, whether you see it, whether you have ever experienced it.

2. **Consider God's track record.** 1 Kings 8:56 says, "Every word has come true of all His good promise, which He promised..." (New Life Version). He has never failed to keep His promises. Fear leaves when you can rely on something that can't fail. There are over 1000 predictions or prophecies in the Bible—promises that God made before they happened. The chances of merely 17 of these coming to pass is ONE out of 450 billion x 1 billion x 1 trillion! Yet, *not one* of these 1000 promised have failed. What does that tell us? God keeps His Word.

3. **Accept the truth that what we fear comes upon us.** In Job 3:25 Job feared that his children would curse God, and that's what happened. When you realize fear has the power to produce negative results, you stop dabbling in it. When a child learns what fire can do, he no longer plays with matches!

4. **Perfect love casts out fear...1 John 4:18.** Flood your mind with thoughts of love—God's love for you, what He was willing to do to rescue you. If He would die for you while you were in sin, separated from God, what wouldn't He do for you? There's just nothing He wouldn't do for you! Think on that, and fear will leave.

5. **There is a promise, from God's Word, for every need you will ever experience.** In fact there are over 7000 promises in the Bible. That's 7000 solutions to life's problems! For example, there is a promise of protection in Psalm 91:1-12, which delivers you from the fear of tragedy.

6. **Pause and think about the fact that God is with you.** Psalm 23:4 says, "...I will fear no evil—for YOU ARE WITH ME." God's presence is the secret to a fear-free life. All fear ultimately is a sense of God's absence, or our separation from God. By contrast, a sense of God's presence delivers us from fear. Hebrews 10:19 says we enter the holy place of His presence by the blood of Jesus. YOU ARE IN HIS PRESENCE, NOW— therefore fear not!

THINK IT & SAY IT

God's Word is true, whether I feel it or not. He has kept all of His promises, and has never failed. Fear leaves me because I rely on something that can't fail—His promises.

What I fear comes upon me, therefore I will fear ONLY GOD, and He will come upon me! God loves me perfectly, and I will not think otherwise, no matter what!

God has made 7000 promises to me, because He knows I need them! God is with me, and therefore I will fear no evil, in Jesus' Name!

Day 17
"I'M AFRAID" (PART II)

Today, we continue destroying thoughts of fear.

1 John 4:18 says "...fear has torment." Perhaps you have felt tormented by the fear of dying, the fear of cancer, the fear of running out of money, or the fear of what someone could do to hurt you. Today, we put an end to the torment, and punishment of fear.

CHANGE IT TODAY

1. **Reject and resist whatever isn't from God.** 2 Timothy 1:7 says, "God has not given you the spirit of fear—but power, love and a sound mind." Fear is from the devil. Don't tolerate it for a second.

2. **Speak to fear—Mark 11:23 says,** "...say to this mountain (of fear) 'be removed and cast into the sea' and do not doubt, but believe those things you say, shall happen." The spoken word has more power than the running thoughts in your head. Speak to those thoughts of fear and command them to go.

3. **Understand how fear comes.** Romans 10:17 says, "FAITH COMES FROM HEARING THE WORD OF GOD." Therefore, FEAR COMES from hearing things contrary to the Word of God. What we hear on the news about tragedy, the economy, etc., is the source of fear. Cut it off at its root. You must spend more time listening to the good news of the Word, rather than the bad news of this world.

4. **Expect to walk on water!** Set your hope and expectation on GREAT things happening in your life. Peter walked on water with Jesus, showing us that faith can overcome anything. However, remember why Peter began to sink. Matthew 14:30—he SAW the wind, he BECAME afraid, he BEGAN to sink. What

we focus on produces fear or faith. FOCUS on the circumstances around you and fear will sink you. FOCUS on the promises of God, and faith will raise you up!

5. **Trust HE will catch you when you fall.** Even when Peter began to sink, Jesus reached out and grabbed His hand to save him. (Matthew 14:31) You always have a safety net in Him! So, fear not!

THINK IT & SAY IT

God has not given me the spirit of fear, but power, love and a sound mind. I reject all forms of fear beginning today. I speak to fear and command it to leave my life and family. I walk by faith, not by sight.

I surrender my ears to listen to God's Word, and my eyes to focus on God promises. I expect the miraculous to happen in my life, and I know God will catch me if I stumble or fall. Therefore, I will not be afraid another day in my life, in Jesus' Name.

Day 18
"I Can't Believe This Is Happening To Me!"

Today we are fasting from the thought that says: "I can't believe this is happening to me!"

When we think this way, we become victims. The devil wants you to live in shock. He wants you to be stopped by the "paralysis of analysis." Folks, every one of us has experienced adversity and trials—a sickness, a sudden break up, a job loss, etc. In **John 16:33**, Jesus said, in this world, you'll have tribulation, but He went on to say the keys to overcoming this way of thinking...

1. **TAKE COURAGE**—How? Realize that He has overcome the world. See yourself as an overcomer. **Romans 8:37** says you are more than a conqueror!

2. **Stop letting life "happen" to you.** And begin to start happening *to life*. The violent take the kingdom by force. **(Matthew 11:12)** Force your faith upon the things that happen to you. Force your faith on your trial.

3. **Confront life.** Stop reacting to it, and get after it! **2 Corinthians 8:1-2** says they overcame their great trial of afflictions with an abundance of joy. Confront trials with joy. They also overcame lack with generosity. Confront lack with giving. It will change!

4. **Focus on what's happening IN YOU, rather than TO YOU.** Jesus could calm the storm AROUND Him, because He had peace and calm WITHIN Him.

Paul said, "We are troubled on every side, but not distressed..." **(2 Corinthians 4:8)** Pressure may come from the outside, but remain fixed on God's Word on the inside. You will come out of every storm!

5. **Remember the power you have in your hand.** Your seeds determine your future **(Galatians 6:7-8).** You can change what happens to you, by changing the seed you sow. For example, sow the seed of treating others right, and you will reap the harvest of being treated right. Sow the seed of giving, and you will reap the harvest of receiving.

THINK IT & SAY IT

I take courage today, because Jesus has overcome the world; therefore I have overcome the world. As He is, so am I in this world! I will no longer be a victim of life, but a victor OVER life. I will happen TO life, rather than the other way around!

I will force my faith upon the things that happen to me, and they will be changed. I confront trials with joy. I develop peace within, by believing God's Word, no matter what is happening on the outside. I have the power to change my future, by the seeds I sow. What happens to me will be transformed by what happens IN me, in Jesus' Name!

Day 19

"PEOPLE ARE
AGAINST ME!"

Today we're fasting from the thought that says: "People are against me."

This thinking stops your love-walk. It's hard to love people that you think are against you. It stops your faith, as well. When you're concerned about what others think, you are not standing on God's promises. Your eyes can't focus on two things at once. When you get your eyes on what others think of you, you take them OFF of what God thinks of you.

CHANGE IT TODAY

1. **Think on what God thinks about you.** Psalm 139:17-18 says, "How precious are Your thoughts toward me, O God. If I could count them, they would outnumber the sands by the seashore."

2. **Realize "even if."** EVEN IF, people are against you, it has NO POWER, because God is for you. Romans 8:31 says, "If God be for us, who can be against us?"

3. **Recognize where the battle is.** NOT AGAINST FLESH AND BLOOD—Ephesians 6:12. We are pulling down strongholds that come from THOUGHTS that oppose the Word of God. DON'T see people as your enemy.

4. **No weapon formed against you can prosper.** (Isaiah 54:17) Condemn every thought that accuses you or threatens you. When a city "condemns" a building, it means you can't live there or build on that property.

Refuse to build upon any thoughts that oppose you or oppose the Word of God.

5. **Stop letting people have so much power in your life.** Jesus is your Lord—you're under His authority, not the authority of others' expectations, plans, or opinions of you.

THINK IT & SAY IT

God's thoughts toward me are precious. His opinion of me is all that matters. He is for me, not against me. EVEN IF people are against me, it doesn't matter. I refuse to give them power over my life. I am under the power of God, and I walk in the power of God.

No weapon formed against me can prosper, because I am the righteousness of God, In Jesus' Name.

Day 20

"WILL I EVER WIN THIS BATTLE?"

Today we are fasting from the thought: "Will I ever win this battle?"

Perhaps you're battling depression, an addiction, or fear. Perhaps it's a sickness or pain. Regardless of what it is, here are the keys to your victory, as we take this thought captive:

1 **YOU'VE ALREADY WON!** Jesus' declaration on the cross sums it up: "It is finished." (John 19:30) What was finished? The battle against the power of sin and the devil. Sin and the devil were defeated that day.

2. **Ask God to open the eyes of your heart** (Ephesians 1:18-19). You must look at life from God's point of view. In 2 Kings 6, when Elisha was surrounded by enemy armies, his servant became afraid and said, 'we're surrounded, what should we do?' Elisha didn't pray for more angels. He prayed: "Lord, open the eyes of my servant, that he would see there are more for us than those against us." (2 Kings 6:16-17) Suddenly, he saw chariots of fire and a host of angels surrounding their enemies! The battle was already won.

3. **Believe you have it!** In Mark 11:24, Jesus said, "That's why I tell you to have faith that you have already received whatever you pray for, and it will be yours." That's power this world can't give you and money can't buy!

Remember 1 Peter 2:24 "...with His stripes you WERE healed." Notice, God speaks to us in past tense. It's already yours!

4. **ONLY BELIEVE.** Stick to what God told you to do! John 6:29 says, 'This is our work: TO BELIEVE.' In other words, BEFORE you pray for rain, bring your umbrella! Expect it to happen. Remember, it's "the good fight of faith." (1 Timothy 6:12) Our job is to believe. Our battle is to believe what God has done, and what is already ours. 2 Chronicles 20:15 says the battle is not yours, but God's.

5. **Praise God that you HAVE the victory.** In 2 Chronicles 20:22 it says, "As they began to sing and praise the Lord, the Lord sent ambushes and their enemies were defeated."

THINK IT & SAY IT

I already have the victory in my life. Jesus has already won my battles for me. My fight is to believe. I refuse to stop believing. I walk by faith and not by sight. I'm the head and not the tail. There are ALREADY more for me than those against me.

I cast my care and trouble on God. He is fighting for me. He is interceding for me right now! I rejoice in the midst of my battles, no matter what things look like. I choose to praise God, in Jesus' Name!

Day 21

"I FEEL SO ANGRY"

Today we are fasting from ANGER – thoughts like "I feel so angry" or "they make me so mad."

Anger is a powerful emotion that obviously can hurt ourselves and others. It leads to bad decisions, damaged relationships, stress and physical sickness. Let's conquer thoughts of anger today!

CHANGE IT TODAY

1. **Discover the power within you.** Remember, anger comes from a sense of powerlessness. When we feel powerless to change something or change *someone*, we get afraid, leading to anger. 2 Timothy 1:7 says God has not given us a spirit of fear, but POWER, love and a sound mind—meditate on this verse.

2. **Listen quickly, speak slowly.** James 1:19 says be quick to hear, slow to speak, THEN, the result: you will be slow to anger!

3. **Realize that anger does not achieve, produce or work!** James 1:20 says, "For the anger of man does not ACHIEVE (WORK, PRODUCE) the righteousness of God." If you had an employee that didn't work, produce or achieve—you would fire them, right? FIRE your anger from your life, it doesn't achieve anything.

4. **Deal with unresolved conflict TODAY!** Ephesians 4:26 says, "Be angry, but do not sin. Do not let the sun go down on your wrath." Make peace with whomever you have something against today. Don't wait.

5. It's OK to feel anger, but direct it the right way—

Notice, the verse goes on to say, "don't give the devil an opportunity to work." The devil wants you to blame others for why you're angry. But REALIZE there's no one to blame, but the slithering devil! And like a machine gun operator who just discovered the enemy, turn it completely on him, use your anger to resist the devil, speaking the Word with an aggressive force, and cut that old dragon to pieces!

THINK IT & SAY IT

I am free from the power of anger. I have power over it. I have power, love and a sound mind. I will not act rashly, but choose to listen quickly and speak slowly.

I "fire" anger from my employment, since it doesn't work, achieve or produce for me. I resolve conflict today and do not let the sun go down on my wrath.

I admit no one is to blame for my angry feelings. I will use what remains of my aggressive feelings against the devil, speaking the Word of God and resisting him FIRMLY in my faith. The violent take the kingdom by force, and that's what I'll do today, in Jesus' Name.

Day 22
"I'm So Depressed"

Building on yesterday's theme, **today we're fasting from the thought that says, "I'm so depressed."** So often, depression is anger turned inward at ourselves for our shortcomings and mistakes.

Perhaps you've thought: "Life's a drag; what's the point of anything; I'll never be happy." These thoughts are designed to rob you of the joy and confidence that produce supernatural strength in our lives.

CHANGE IT TODAY

1. **Stop condemning yourself.** Condemnation is a mindset that robs you of joy and peace. Romans 14:22 says, "Happy is the man who does not condemn himself..."

2. **God's still working on you!** Lighten up on yourself. Philippians 1:6 says, He began a good work in you; He'll finish it! Trust God that you're making progress. You're not standing still.

3. **Tap into the power of believing.** 1 Peter 1:8 says "...though you do not see Him now, you BELIEVE in Him, and are filled with inexpressible and glorious joy." (AMP) Believe the promise of God regardless of what you see, and depression will begin to leave.

4. **Recognize and eliminate negative thoughts, one at a time.** For example, if you think "this will never work," replace it immediately with: "It will work, because God is taking care of whatever concerns me." (Psalm 138:8)

5. **Surround yourself with positive people.** Positive thinking and speaking is contagious, just as negative thinking is. Be around only those who create an atmosphere of victory with their words.

6. **Remember, you are not helpless.** Thoughts of helplessness bring depression. The Holy Spirit is our Helper (John 14:16-18; John 15:26; John 16:7).

THINK IT & SAY IT

I will never be depressed another day in my life. I decide to stop condemning myself and beating myself up for my shortcomings. I believe God is working on me every day.

I am not a negative thinker. I am positive. God is for me, with me and in me, therefore depression cannot stay. I command every ounce of depression to loose me and let me go, be removed and cast into the sea, in Jesus' Name!

Day 23
"WHAT AM I GOING TO DO?"

Today we're fasting from the thought that says, **"What am I going to do?"** Or **"I don't know how I'm going to make it."**

Listen to the profound words of Jesus in Matthew 6:25 when He said, **"Take NO THOUGHT"** saying, 'What shall you eat or what shall you drink; or what shall you wear...' Notice, Jesus says we are not to accept these thoughts.

CHANGE IT TODAY

1. **Jesus knew that the thought life is where the battle is decided.**

2. **Our thoughts produce POWER when we speak them out loud.** That's why Jesus said, "Take no thought, SAYING..." We take negative thoughts into our lives when we speak them out loud.

3. **Cast all your cares on God.** (1 Peter 5:7) He knows you need all these things; and He will take care of it, when you turn it over to Him.

4. **Expect God to speak to you.** When you don't know what to do, listen to your heart. Be still. You will hear God's voice (1 Kings 19:11-12, John 10:27).

5. **See Him as YOUR God.** Paul said, "My God shall supply..." When you know He is YOUR God, you will trust Him to supply. Psalm 91:2 says, "You shall SAY of the Lord: You are my refuge, my fortress, MY GOD, in YOU do I trust!"

6. **Seek His kingdom—His way of doing things.** (Mark 4:26 says the Kingdom of God is like a man planting seed.) You're going to make it because you plant the seed of God's Word in your heart.

THINK IT & SAY IT

When I don't know what to do, I will trust God to lead me. I expect God to speak to me. His still, small voice will be clear to me today.

He is MY God. He shall supply my every need. I seek the Kingdom of God and His righteousness, and all the things missing in my life will be added to me, in Jesus' Name!

"WHAT MIGHT HAVE BEEN"

I hope you're encouraged as we are getting to the root of thinking that has kept us from all that God has for us.

Remember, success or failure in life is created by how we think.

Today we're fasting from the thought: "What might have been." So often we allow thoughts of regret to paralyze us from a happy and victorious present and future. Today we get rid of the "woulda, shoulda, coulda" mentality. (I shoulda gone to college; I coulda made it, if I had the right breaks; I woulda succeeded if someone would have given me a break...")

CHANGE IT TODAY

1. **Forget what might have been, and look forward to what CAN BE.** Faith in the possibilities of God extinguishes regret. Ephesians 6:16 says the shield of faith quenches all the fiery darts of the wicked one.

2. **Meditate on Philippians 3:13-14** which says, "...this one thing I do, forgetting what lies behind, reaching forward to what lies ahead, I press on toward the goal..." Notice 3 words: forgetting, reaching, pressing. **Forgetting** means: **forego** what you can't get back. Don't hold on to your regrets. Give them to God.

3. **Recognize God has something better for you.** Hebrews 11:40 says, "God has something better for us." Expect it. Look forward to it.

4. **Take charge of what CAN BE with your words.** Job 22:28 says, "You shall decree a thing, and it shall be established to you..."

5. **Just Do It.** Start doing, *today*, what you should have done yesterday (provided it's godly!) It's never too late! Psalm 118:24 says THIS IS THE DAY the Lord has made—let us rejoice—take ACTION. Daniel 11:32 says, "Those who know their God will be strong and TAKE ACTION, DO EXPLOITS..."

THINK IT & SAY IT

Today I give up the 'woulda, shoulda, coulda' mentality. I will not ask 'what might have been.' I'll declare what is and what will be with my words. I forget what lies behind and refuse to look back anymore at what I missed out on or could have had. I give up regret forever.

God has something better for me today, and I accept it, take action toward it, and expect the greatest days of my life ahead—in Jesus' Name.

Day 25

"GOD IS NOT ANSWERING MY PRAYERS"

Today we're fasting from the thought that says: "God is not answering my prayers." This mentality prevents us from receiving all that God has for us.

Let's overcome this today by renewing our minds to what God REALLY says about prayer.

CHANGE IT TODAY

1. **Pray the Word of God.** God's Word was God's idea! So He intends for it to come to pass. 1 John 5:14-15 says, "If we ask anything according to His will (His Word) we know He hears us...and we know we have whatever we've asked." John 15:7 says, "If you abide in Me and My Words abide in you, ask whatever you wish and it SHALL be done for you."

2. **God always says "Yes" to His Word—His promises.** 2 Corinthians 1:20 says, "All the promises of God are yes, in Him, and with us is the 'Amen'." There is total assurance that prayer will be answered if it's not something God has already promised in His Word.

3. **Walk by faith** (2 Corinthians 5:7). Regardless of how you feel, faith says: God has heard me, and He answers. Mark 11:24 says, "Believe you HAVE received...and it shall be granted to you."

4. **Don't throw in the towel when you don't see it working.** Hebrews 6:12 says, "...through faith AND patience, we inherit the promises of God."

5. **Apply the secret of Persistence** (Luke 18:1-8).
   Matthew 7:7 (AMP) says, "Keep on asking and it will
   be given...keep on knocking and the door will
   be opened."

6. **Don't let condemnation rob you of your confidence.**
   1 John 3:20-22 says, "...If our heart does not condemn
   us—THERE IS NO CONDEMNATION FOR THOSE WHO
   ARE IN CHRIST JESUS—then we have confidence
   toward God; and whatever we ask we receive..."

THINK IT & SAY IT

God DOES answer my prayers. No matter what I see or feel,
I walk by faith, and not by sight. Condemnation for my mistakes or shortcomings will not rob me of confidence. God is
bigger than my mistakes.

His Word abides in me, and therefore I can ask and receive. I won't be discouraged or give up, because I will
reap if I do not faint. My answer is coming! In Jesus' Name!

Day 26
"I'll Never Recover From This"

Whether it's a financial crisis you're in, or a divorce you've been through, or an unthinkable sin you've committed, don't ever give in to the thinking that you won't recover. Nothing's more discouraging than to think you'll never get out of the pain, debt or guilt you're in. Let's fast from this.

CHANGE IT TODAY

1. **God always provides a way of escape.** No matter what you're facing, there's a way out (1 Corinthians 10:13). In fact, Jesus IS the WAY.

2. **Get this in your thinking: WHATEVER GOD DID FOR THEM (in scripture), HE'LL DO FOR YOU!** He is no respecter of persons (Romans 2:11). Elijah recovered from financial crisis. Jacob recovered from marriage problems. David recovered from unthinkable sins, etc.

3. **YOU SHALL RECOVER ALL!** That's a promise that God made to David when he lost everything in his life. Stand on it. 1 Samuel 30:8 says, "You shall surely overtake them and you shall recover all."

4. **IT IS GOD'S WILL FOR YOU TO RECOVER.** In John 10:10 Jesus says, "The thief came to steal, kill and destroy, but I have come that you would have life in abundance, to the full, till it overflows!"

5. **Get your focus on praying for others' recovery.** Job 42:10 says, "The LORD restored the fortunes of Job when he prayed for his friends, and the LORD increased all that Job had twofold."

THINK IT & SAY IT

I will recover all that has been lost, stolen or missing from my life. I will recover from whatever sin or addiction I've faced. God did it for David, Job, Elijah—He'll do it for me. There is always a way, and I receive the wisdom from God to find it now.

Jesus came to restore everything back to me as God intended. I receive at least double back for everything that I have ever lost, in Jesus' Name.

Day 27

"I DESERVE THE PAIN I'M GOING THROUGH"

Many people remain hurt and defeated in life because they think they deserve what's happened to them. People who have been abused, for example, often think it was their fault, or they had it coming. As a result, they accept their situation and never mount the faith to overcome it.

CHANGE IT TODAY

1. **Other people's actions are NOT your fault.** REALIZE people do what they do because of their own inner pain, dysfunction, and bad choices, **not because of you**. Stop feeling like the "mama of someone else's drama."

2. **Embrace the truth that Jesus bore your pain.** Isaiah 53:4-5 says, "He Himself bore our sickness and pain and with His stripes we are healed." If He bore it, **you shouldn't have to!**

3. **Meditate on Romans 8:32**—"He that did not spare His own Son, but delivered Him up for us all, **how shall He not also with Him, freely give us all things.**" Through Jesus' sacrifice, you deserve everything He paid for you to have—spirit, soul, body, finances, relationships—**all things!**

4. **Realize torment, pain and suffering are from the devil!** Do not think for a moment that God wants you to suffer in these ways. John 10:10 says, "the thief comes to steal, kill and destroy..." Acts 10:38 says, "...Jesus went about...healing ALL that were oppressed OF THE DEVIL."

5. **YOU DO NOT DESERVE THE PAIN AND SUFFERING THAT JESUS PAID THE PRICE FOR.** RESIST IT!
(1 Peter 5:8, James 4:7)

THINK IT & SAY IT

I do not deserve the pain and suffering that Jesus already paid the price for. I did deserve it, but He took it; and I refuse to tolerate it or accept it another day in my life. What people have wrongly done to me is not my fault and not my burden to figure out. I am healed from it, by the stripes of Jesus. God freely gives me all things, because He did not withhold His own Son.

God loves me and desires to bless me with all of the promises of His Word. He says I DO deserve it, because I believe in His covenant, in Jesus' Name!

Day 28

"I'm Not Going To Make It"

Today we're fasting from the thought: "I'm not going to make it." So often these thoughts fill our minds: we might not make it financially, we might not make it through this marriage problem, through this sickness, this trial, etc.

CHANGE IT TODAY

1. **God is faithful.** He didn't bring you this far to leave you now. Philippians 1:6 says He began this work in you, He will finish it.

2. **Remember, faith finds a way** (Mark 2:4-5). God will always provide a way for you to make it.

3. **You have favor.** Psalm 5:12 says favor surrounds you like a shield. Revelation 3:7-8 says God will open a door that no man can shut. Expect favor.

4. **Trust Him to carry you.** Deuteronomy 1:31 says, "There you saw how the LORD your God carried you, as a father carries his son, all the way you went until you reached this place." He loves you. He will carry you through this.

5. **You have the wisdom of God** (1 Corinthians 2:16). With the mind of Christ, you will figure out how to make it.

6. **Believe in the power of praise.** James 1:2 says, "Count it all joy when you encounter various trials." Look up Acts 16:25-26

THINK IT & SAY IT

I am going to make it. I am going to make it emotionally. I am going to make it financially. I am going to make it through everything I'm facing or ever will face. God brought me this far, He will lead me all the way.

God will open a door for me to make it. He will carry me when I'm weary. I will praise my way through this and will find a way, in Jesus' Name!

Day 29

"WE CAN'T EXPECT TO EXPERIENCE THE MIRACLES OF THE BIBLE TODAY"

Today we are fasting from the thought: "The power and miracles in the Bible are great, but we can't expect to experience those today!"

Many people also think: "We can't have the faith that Paul had or Peter, etc." These are thoughts that don't necessarily pop into our heads, but they are mindsets ingrained in us, undermining our ability to believe for the impossible to become possible. If you adopt these beliefs, they will keep you living below your God-given privileges.

CHANGE IT TODAY

1. **We HAVE, right now, the same faith** that the early apostles had. In 2 Peter 1:1 Peter writes, "...to those who have received like precious faith with us by the righteousness of our God and our Savior Jesus Christ."

2. **Understand the source of this faith and power in our lives: the righteousness of God.** This is a free gift (2 Corinthians 5:17, 21). It's not because of the times we're living in, it's because we are the righteousness of God.

3. **There's nothing He's holding back from you.** 2 Peter 1:3 says, "His divine power has granted to us everything pertaining to life and godliness."

4. **The power and promises are already yours.** 2 Peter 1:4 says, "He HAS GRANTED TO US His precious and magnificent promises..."

5. **You have the same Spirit** that Jesus had when He was in this world (Romans 8:11).

6. **Expect to walk in this power.** In John 14:12 Jesus said, "The works that I do, shall you do also, and greater works shall you do..." He also said in Mark 16, "these signs shall follow THOSE WHO BELIEVE..." **BELIEVE TODAY!**

THINK IT & SAY IT

I have received faith OF THE SAME KIND as the apostles, because I am the righteousness of God in Jesus Christ. He has granted to me already EVERYTHING pertaining to life and godliness. That includes every area of my life.

God's power and promises are already mine. I expect to walk in His divine power through His divine nature working in me today, in Jesus' Name."

Day 30
GET RID OF
BACKWARD THINKING

Today, we're fasting from backward thinking. So often, we start our days, or our prayers with WHAT WE DON'T HAVE. Around the world today, people are focused on what they don't have, and trying to figure out how to get it. This is what I mean by "backward thinking."

Anything good that is going to happen in our lives today, starts with getting our minds on what we ALREADY have, not what we don't have.

CHANGE IT TODAY

1. **THINK BACK, but NOT backward.** Every day, we need to THINK about the things God has already done. In Psalm 103:1-5 David said, "...forget none of His benefits: He pardons your sins, heals all your diseases, redeems your life from destruction, crowns you with lovingkindness and compassion..." Make a list—it will change how you look at your life.

2. **Focus on the 'prayer of thanksgiving'.** Start EVERY prayer thanking God for what He has already done for you (Philippians 4:6-7). This creates FAITH ENERGY. As you reflect on what God has specifically given you already, it awakens your ability to believe for more.

3. **Meditate on Philemon vs. 6.** "Your faith becomes effective, as you acknowledge every good thing already in you, through Christ Jesus."

4. **Step out of the comparison trap.** 2 Corinthians 10:12 says, "when we compare ourselves with one another, we misunderstand life." Confusion, misunderstanding, and jealousy all set in when we measure ourselves with what others have or do.

5. **Develop selective memory.** Think back ONLY on the good that has happened in your life. FORGET the pain. Let go of the hurts and losses you've suffered (Philippians 3:13).

6. **Expect God to make up to you the years** that have been lost through your pains, mistakes and wrong ways of thinking. In Joel 2:23-25 God said, "I will restore the years that have been devoured..."

THINK IT & SAY IT

I focus my prayer and start my day with what God has already done in my life. I will bless the Lord at all times, His praise shall continually be in my mouth. I am already complete in Jesus Christ.

I choose to focus on thanking God for what He has already done in my life. I adopt an attitude of gratitude.

I give up comparing myself to others, and I expect God to make up to me all that I have lost through years of backward thinking, In Jesus' Name.

Day 31
"If I Only Had This One Thing, Life Would Be So Much Easier"

Today we're fasting from the thought: **"If I only had this one thing, life would be so much easier (so much better)."**

We always seem to be ONE THING short of happiness or fulfillment (the right person, career, help, assistance, home, etc.). Today, we need to get rid of this type of thinking. The problem with it is—it is a lie! As soon as you get the one thing that you think you're missing, something else will come up.

CHANGE IT TODAY

1. **Remember Adam and Eve.** (Genesis 3:1-6) GOD GAVE THEM ALL THE TREES to eat of, freely. THEY FOCUSED ON THE ONE THEY COULDN'T have. Had THEY EATEN FREELY from the other ones, they would have been satisfied. Eat of God's Word, love, and grace—you will be satisfied!

2. **You have the ultimate Helper—the Holy Spirit.** (John 16:13) He will help you accomplish God's perfect will for your life.

3. **Expect the Holy Spirit to help your weaknesses and strengthen you.** (Romans 8:26) He intercedes for us, prays for us, does our praying IN us.

4. **Discover NOW the secret of contentment:** Philippians 4:11-13, "No matter the circumstances around me," Paul said, "I can do all things through Christ which strengthens me." You CAN make it through life without the thing you are missing—you have the ANOINTED ONE living inside of you!

5. **Shift your focus.** God commanded not to covet; but it wasn't because He didn't want you to have everything good. It's that He didn't want you to focus on what you didn't have. YOU HAVE ALL THINGS pertaining to life and godliness (2 Peter 1:3). SPEND YOUR TIME THINKING ABOUT WHAT IS ALREADY YOURS IN CHRIST JESUS!

THINK IT & SAY IT

I eat freely of God's Word, His love, and His grace, and I am satisfied! The Holy Spirit will help whatever is weak or lacking in my life. I can make it through anything and live in any condition, because the Anointed One lives in me. He has supplied my every need, giving me all things pertaining to life and godliness.

I am not one thing short of being happy. I am blessed, happy, fortunate and to be envied, because God has favored me. Therefore, I lack no good thing, in Jesus' Name!

Day 32

GET RID OF NEGATIVITY

Negative thinking produces negative results, negative relationships, negative emotions and even negative physical
symptoms. Negative thoughts come when we see ourselves defeated, beaten down, betrayed, unwanted, or of
no value. (Thoughts like: I will never be successful, I can't
do anything right, people will never change, etc., all come
from a negative view of ourselves and life.)

CHANGE IT TODAY

1. **Think of yourself as God thinks of you.** You are the
   head, not the tail, above ONLY and not beneath
   (Deut. 28:13). This is where negativity begins to FLEE!

2. **Whenever a negative thought comes to mind,
   deliberately overcome it BY VOICING a positive
   one.** Example: When the thought comes, "I'll never
   make it through this," DECLARE OUT LOUD: "I am an
   overcomer, and I can do all things through Christ."

3. **Create FAITH ENERGY.** Faith comes from HEARING the
   Word (Romans 10:17). You hear the Word every time
   you SPEAK the Word. 2 Corinthians 4:13 says, "having
   the same spirit of faith, we believed, therefore, we
   SPEAK..."

4. **FIRE your negative attitudes, like they were
   destructive employees. Admit negative attitudes
   NEVER produce good.** When you stay aligned with
   these attitudes, you produce negative power. Jesus
   said in Matthew 18:19, "If two agree, it shall be done."

When you think negatively, you are agreeing with the devil, the naysayers, and the doom and gloom prognosticators, producing power for those things to come to pass.

5. **Agree with God.** Whether you feel it or not, see it or not, demand of yourself to speak words of victory from the scripture that God has amply supplied you with (Deut. 28:2-14, Romans 8:31-38, Philippians 4:4-8).

THINK IT & SAY IT

I think of myself God's way: I am the head and not the tail, I am above, not beneath; I am blessed coming in and going out. I deliberately overcome negative thoughts by voicing positive ones from the Word of God.

I release the spirit of faith in my life by believing and speaking God's Word. I fire negative attitudes and command them to leave my life. I agree with God that I am victorious in all things and more than a conqueror, in Jesus' Name!

Day 33
GET RID OF SMALL THINKING

Most people probably wouldn't even consider "small thinking" to be a sin. That's where we have to change our thinking FIRST. If we set up small and limited expectations of ourselves and our lives, that's what we'll get. The problem with that is God has so much more for us.

CHANGE IT TODAY

1. **Think big!** Renew your mind to God's language. For example: "Ask for the nations" (Psalm 2); "Speak to the mountain" (Mark 11); "your descendants shall be as numerous as the stars" (Genesis 15); "you shall possess the land" (Numbers 13), etc. God uses BIG language to give us big dreams.

2. **Ask for what you want; don't settle for what you get.** Ephesians 3:20 says, "God is able to do exceeding abundantly beyond all that we can ask or think." Start asking and thinking the way God says to.

3. **Never stop dreaming and envisioning a better life.** In Acts 2:17 God says "In the last days I will pour out my Spirit upon all people... Your young men will see visions, and your old men will dream dreams." You never grow old until dreams begin to be replaced by regrets. Never stop dreaming.

4. **Don't be afraid of failure and disappointment.** If you shoot for the stars and end up on the moon, at least you've made progress. Never stop trying.

5. **Take your seat!** What do I mean? God has seated us with Jesus Christ in heavenly places (Ephesians 2:6). We have been given a divine authority and divine point of view. That's how we need to look at life. We are already positioned ABOVE our wildest dreams and expectations, so let's go get them!

THINK IT & SAY IT

I give up small thinking. I agree with God's way of looking at things, and God's language. I decide to think bigger and bigger every day, and to ask for the things God said I could ask for.

I accept the visions and dreams that the Holy Spirit wants to give me, and I let go of all fear-based small thoughts. I will not stop dreaming. I will not stop trying. I have divine authority and am seated with Christ in heavenly places. I am bigger than the mountains because I am made in the image of God. I think bigger, dream bigger and expect bigger today. The Greater One lives in me and has given me the power to see His visions and dreams fulfilled in my life, in Jesus' Name!

Day 34
"I've Reached My Limit"

Today we're fasting from the thought that says: "I've reached my limit (my ceiling)."

How many times have we felt like we've reached our limit? "I can't make it any further." "I can't take it anymore." Perhaps you feel you can't advance any further based on your experience, education, or expectation.

CHANGE IT TODAY

1. **ENLARGE your capacity to receive.** Realize there is MORE that God has for you, and get ready to receive it. Isaiah 54:2 says, "Make wide the place of your tent, and let the curtains of your house be stretched out without limit: make your cords long, and your tent-pins strong."

2. **Ask for more of whatever you need.** James 4:1-2 says, "You have not, because you ask not." John 16:24 says, "Ask and you shall receive—that your joy may be made full."

3. **Believe you have received it, the moment you ask** (Mark 11:24). And it will be yours!

4. **Take the limits off of what God can and WILL do in your life.** Psalm 78:41 says, "they tempted God and they limited the Holy One of Israel." How did they limit Him? Verse 42 says, "They did not remember His power." REMEMBER what God has already done.

5. **Magnify the Lord.** Psalm 34:3 says meditate on how big God is. The bigger you see Him, the bigger you'll see yourself, because you are made in His image (Genesis 1:26-28).

6. **LET THE WEAK SAY, "I AM STRONG."** (Joel 3:10) No matter how weak or limited you feel, DECLARE "I am strong!"

THINK IT & SAY IT

I enlarge my capacity to receive. There's so much more God can give me and do in my life. I can make it further; I can handle much more in life. I expect God's ability to strengthen me.

I will not limit God by my previous experiences, but I will remember all the miracles He has already done. I declare 'I am strong' in the Lord and the power of His might. I can go to God and receive more of whatever I need—and I receive it, in Jesus' Name!

Day 35

OUR WORDS DON'T HAVE THAT MUCH POWER

As we come close to the end of this 40 day fast from wrong thinking, I encourage you to use these meditations as a resource you can come back to ANYTIME the negative thoughts comes back. Develop the habit of stopping wrong thinking continually, and you will see amazing results.

Today, we're fasting from the mentality that "our words don't have that much power." We often think "what I SAY doesn't really matter" or "speaking God's Word doesn't work for me."

These mindsets have defeated us far too long.

CHANGE IT TODAY

1   **Death and life are in the power of the tongue** (Proverbs 18:21).

2. **True satisfaction and happiness come from speaking fruitful words** (Proverbs 18:20).

3. **"Believing and speaking" are God's way of getting things done.** We're saved by believing and confessing Jesus as Lord (Romans 10:9-10). If the greatest gift of salvation is received in this way, everything else should follow suit.

4. **Everything God created came from WORDS** (Genesis 1:1-31). "And God SAID, "Let there be light, and light was."

5. **We're made in His image. SPEAK HIS WORDS.** Paul said, "It is written, 'I believed, therefore I have spoken.' With that same spirit of faith WE ALSO believe and therefore SPEAK." (2 Corinthians 4:13)

6. **Store up God's Word in your heart, and power will come forth** (Luke 6:45).

7. **It doesn't work unless we speak according to His will** (1 John 5:14). BUT HIS WILL IS CLEARLY WRITTEN—His Will is His Word. You can't say, "I command my boss to get hit by a bus on the way to work!" There is no scripture to support speaking things like that, even when you feel them! But you can declare, "I have favor at my job, and peace with all men..." You get the point!

THINK IT & SAY IT

I give up the thought that my words don't matter. My words have power. They bring me life and satisfaction. I will employ God's method of getting things done, by believing and speaking His Word.

I am made in His image, and therefore my Words bring things to pass. I believe, therefore I speak, and good things comes forth, in Jesus' Name.

Day 36
OUR WORDS DON'T HAVE THAT MUCH POWER (PART II)

...More on "words." Today, I want us to continue to fast from the mistaken belief that our words don't have power. Remember, death and life are in the power of the tongue (Proverbs 18:21). James 3:4-5 says that our words steer and set the course of our lives.

CHANGE IT TODAY

1. **Believe what Jesus said in Mark 11:23**, "Whoever shall say to this mountain, 'be removed and cast into the sea', and does not doubt, but believes that those things which he says shall come to pass; he shall have whatever he says." **Those who understand the power of the spoken Word shall have what they say.**

2. **Believe the things you say WILL come to pass.** Another way that "faith energy" is created is by believing that when you say something, it has the power to come to pass.

3. **It's natural and supernatural.** We use words to CREATE a romantic mood. We use words to create sales in business. God set it up for our words to be a creative force.

4. **Words are seeds.** They are designed to grow when planted, whether they are bad or good. Mark 4:14 says, "The sower sows the Word." Pay careful attention to the things you say, because they have

the power to come to pass. SPEAK THE WORD ONLY (Matthew 8:8).

5. **Realize the Holy Spirit is waiting on us to speak God's Word.** Genesis 1:2-3 says, "...and the Spirit of God was hovering over the face of the waters. Then God said, "Let there be light. And there was light." Notice, the Holy Spirit was hovering, brooding, waiting to give birth to something. But nothing happened until God SPOKE. The Holy Spirit is hovering, waiting in our lives. When we speak God's Word, the same Holy Spirit uses those words to bring those things to pass.

6. **Acts 10:44-45 says, "While Peter was speaking the Word, the Holy Spirit fell on those who were listening."** Notice, it was the words he spoke that gave the Holy Spirit something to work with.

THINK IT & SAY IT

I believe that my words set the course of my life. I believe the things which I say will come to pass. I use my words as seeds to plant God's will in my life. As I speak God's Word, I give the Holy Spirit room to work in my life and my situations, in Jesus' Name.

Day 37

"I WILL NEVER HAVE GREAT SUCCESS"

Today we're fasting from the thought: "I will never have great success". Deep in our minds lies a subtle, if not obvious, tolerance of mediocrity and "just getting by." God has so much more for us! Let's walk in it.

1. **Abundant success is truly God's will for your life.** Psalm 35:27 says, "God DELIGHTS (takes pleasure) in the prosperity/success of His servants."

2. **Expect success in EVERY area of life.** Deuteronomy 28:8 says, "The LORD will command the blessing upon you in your barns and in all that you put your hand to, and He will bless you in the land which the LORD your God gives you."

3. **You have a covenant with God!** Deuteronomy 29:9 says, "So keep the words of this covenant to do them that **you may prosper in all** that you do."

4. **God's Word contains the seeds of true success.** Joshua 1:8 says, **Never stop declaring this Word**, "but you shall meditate on it day and night, so that you may be careful to do according to all that is written in it; for then you will make your way prosperous, and then you will have good success."

5. **Success comes from God's presence.** Genesis 39:2 says, "For the Lord was WITH Joseph, so he became a successful man." Meditate on the fact that GOD IS WITH YOU. 1 Chronicles 22:11 says, "Now, my son, **the LORD be with you that you may be successful.**"

THINK IT & SAY IT

God takes pleasure in my abundant success and prosperity in life. He commands the blessing in everything I put my hand to. I have a covenant with God and therefore I trust that I will prosper in all that I do.

I will never stop believing and speaking the Word of God which brings true success. God's presence in my life guarantees great success in my life today and every day, in Jesus' Name.

Day 38
EXCUSE-MAKING MENTALITIES

Today we are going to eliminate excuse-making mentalities. Sometimes people think, "If people wouldn't have treated me like that, I would be successful" or "if my problem was anything other than this, I could handle it." You probably know countless other thoughts that are similar.

CHANGE IT TODAY

1. Refuse to excuse mediocrity. 1 Thessalonians 4:1 says "... Excel still more..." Don't give in to the temptation to settle. Wherever you're at in life right now, thank God but then press forward for more of what God has for you.

2. Refuse to excuse sickness. Don't tolerate it, saying it runs in your family or it's a cross to bear, or everyone gets sick. He sent His Word and healed us (Psalm 107:20). With His stripes, we are healed (1 Peter 2:24).

3. Refuse to excuse lack and failure in your life, Stop thinking that you were born on the wrong side of the tracks or you're limited by your upbringing. You may have been born on the wrong side of the tracks, but you're not bound to stay there. Cross the tracks NOW (Romans 8:37).

4. Refuse to excuse unforgiveness. Stop saying, "You just don't know what they did to me." God knows what WE did to HIM and He still forgives.

5. Refuse to excuse lack of support. In John 5:7 the lame man said, "I have no man to help me." He used that as an excuse to remain in his condition. Even if everyone lets us down, God will support us (Psalm 27:10).

6. Refuse to excuse sin, saying, "I just can't overcome it...." YOU CAN do all things through Christ which strengthens you (Philippians 4:13). You have been given power over the enemy. 1 Corinthians 15:34 says, "Awake to righteousness and you'll stop sinning." When you realize you ARE the righteousness of God, made right with Him, BY Him, you experience a power that delivers you from the power of sin.

THINK IT & SAY IT

I eliminate excuse-making from my thoughts and words. I will no longer excuse or justify mediocrity in my life. I will not excuse sickness. I am healed by Jesus' stripes.

I will not excuse failure, as God declares I am more than a conqueror. I am forgiven and I will not withhold forgiveness from others. God takes up my cause and is my greatest support. I have received the gift of righteousness, giving me the power to stop sinning, and walk in my divine authority, in Jesus' Name!

Day 39

"THERE IS SO MUCH WRONG IN MY LIFE"

Today we're fasting from the thought that says:

"There is so much wrong in my life how can I ever expect anything good to come my way?"

CHANGE IT TODAY

1. **Believe! God honors faith, even when we have fallen or failed.** Galatians 3:9 says, "We are blessed with Abraham the believer." Blessed are those who believe. Good comes to those who believe.

2. **Every good gift comes from the Father** (James 1:17). God is your Father. He will take care of you because you are His beloved (Mark 1:11).

3. **Goodness and mercy will follow you all the days of your life** (Psalm 23:6). ALL THE DAYS OF YOUR LIFE include the days that you have had so much wrong in your life.

4. **Know that you're forgiven and redeemed from the curse** (Galatians 3:13). You're not blessed because of the right or wrong in your life. You're blessed because Jesus took the curse upon Himself and gave us the blessing. There was much wrong in Abraham's life; but he believed God, and it was reckoned to him as righteousness. That's when the blessing flowed!

5. **God blesses us because of His love for us**
   (Deut. 7:7-8). The Lord did not set His love upon you because of you, but because He loved you and kept the oath which he swore to your forefathers. His blessings are the overflow of His love. Believe it!

6. **Stop condemning yourself. God's promises are greater than our mistakes** (1 John 3:20-21). There is no condemnation for those in Christ (Romans 8:1).

THINK IT & SAY IT

Even though there is wrong in my life, God is greater than my heart and greater than my mistakes. His blood cleanses me and brings me into His blessing. I'm blessed with Abraham the believer.

I'm redeemed from the curse of negativity and failure. Goodness and mercy will follow me, because the Lord is my shepherd. I expect to receive every good and perfect gift from my heavenly Father, in Jesus' Name.

Day 40

"It's Just So Hard To Trust God"

As we conclude this phase of our FAST FROM WRONG THINKING, I am grateful for the opportunity to minister to you in this unique way.

Today we're fasting from the thought that "It's just so hard to trust God." "God's promises don't always work."

So often, trusting someone is the hardest thing to do. But why do we withhold our trust from others? Because often, they have developed a track record that cannot be relied upon.

God, on the other hand, has a much better track record. He has never broken His promises!

Let's fast from this thinking that it's hard to trust God.

CHANGE IT TODAY

1. **The foundation for trusting someone is a proven track record of integrity.** If they have kept their word as a pattern in their life, you can trust them to do it again. This confidence produces trust.

2. **Look at the facts:** 1 Kings 8:56 says, "...not one word has failed of all His good promise." God has NEVER broken His promise. He can be trusted!

3. **Ponder this amazing statistic:** There are over 1000 prophecies in the Bible—promises that God made before they happened.

The chances of merely 17 of these coming to pass is ONE out of 450 billion x 1 billion x 1 trillion! Yet, *not one* of these 1000 promised have failed.

4. **It is impossible for God to lie** (Hebrews 6:18). If God were to lie or break His promise, He would become subject to the devil (the father of lies—John 8:44), and forfeit His throne. That's something He will NEVER do.

5. **All His promises are available to you today!**
   2 Corinthians 1:20 says, "For as many as are the promises of God, in Him they are YES! And with us is the 'Amen' (SO BE IT!)." Pray His promises. Receive, by faith, His promises. Expect His promises to come to pass in your life.

THINK IT & SAY IT

I trust the Lord with all my heart, because He has never broken His promise. Not one of His words has failed. It is impossible for Him to lie. Whatever God has promised in His Word, His answer is YES to me because I am in Christ. I stand on His promises, one by one, and declare "Amen", "So be it", in Jesus' Name!"

CONCLUSION

Now that you've begun this REVOLUTION—From the Inside Out, let me encourage you with a few final thoughts.

1. **Review regularly.** Don't let up. The devil will try to make you fall back into wrong thinking. Whenever a negative thought comes back, go back and review how to overcome this thought from that particular day.

2. **Share your testimony.** Something else that will keep you walking in victory is sharing how God has changed your life. Please send me your testimony at www.thinkingfast.org. This will encourage someone else to know that their life can be changed too!

3. **Help me take this revolution to the world.** God has called us to change the world, one life at a time, one thought at a time. This a big job, but remember, Nothing is impossible to those who believe. Lets think big, and believe big! You can help me take this revolutionary message to millions of others around the world by sowing a seed of any amount. Just log onto www.thinkingfast.org and click on "Make a Donation." Stand with me in getting the word out about this life-changing fast from wrong thinking.

4. **Finally, don't ever forget:** There is no stopping the man or woman who is set free from wrong thinking. Remember, "As a man thinks within, so is he!" (Proverbs 23:7)